I0487235

Digital Photography

Understanding The Unique World Of Digital Photography

By

Renee B. Williams

Renee B. Williams

Digital Photography

Renee B. Williams

Digital Photography

ACKNOWLEDGMENTS

For my students and friends, who all selflessly helped me in writing this book. Special thanks to those who asked, insisted and assisted me in turning the seminars **in** this practical form. All Rights Reserved 2012-2015 @ Renee B. Williams.

Renee B. Williams

TABLE OF CONTENTS

Digital Photography

- **Staying Honest To Your Business And Clients**
- **Never Make Rush Decisions**
- **Be Ready To Train Others To Work With You**

Chapter 3 - How Digital Photography Benefits The World

Chapter 4 - Understanding The 5 W's Of Digital Photography

- **What**
- **Who**
- **When**
- **Where**
- **Whom**

Chapter 5 - Digital Photography For Fun

Chapter 6 - Digital Photography For Events

- **Weddings**

- **Corporate Parties**
- **Birthday Parties**
- **Concerts**
- **Graduations**
- **Funerals**
- **Naming Ceremonies**

Chapter 7 - Building Your Confidence As A Digital Photographer

Chapter 8 - Digital Photography Cameras

- **Benefits of Using High Quality Cameras**
- **Where To Find Information About Different Digital Cameras**
- **Cameras For Professional And Hobby Pictures**
- **Smartphone Cameras**
- **Compact Digital Cameras**

Chapter 9 - Digital Photography In All Industries

Digital Photography

Renee B. Williams

Chapter 13 - Learning Digital Photography

- **Online Digital Photography Classes**
- **Choosing The Right Courses**
- **Paying The Right Amount For The Education You Get**
- **Read Online Reviews To Help You Decide**
- **Always Compare Different Online Teaching Sites**
- **Free Online Digital Photography Courses**

FAQ

Disclaimer

About Author

INTRODUCTION

Although you might have not thought about it so much, digital photography has, in a huge amount changed our lives in so many unique ways. It is true that one of those unique ways has to do with the ease it has brought where taking pictures are concerned there are many other benefits. Our lives have been improved in so many ways with the digital world taking center stage. If you love to take pictures and love to keep memories in the pictures you take, there will be the need for you to understand better what digital photography is and how simple shots with your phones can transform the way you live your life.

In this Book, you will get to comprehend all there is to understand about digital photography and also benefit from the vast intelligence that knowing more about this world of arts has to offer. Today, more and more people are gaining high interest both financially and emotionally with the uniqueness, digital photographs offer and how clear-cut they are. Reading and understanding the information provided in this Book will make it very easy for you to become one of the best digital photographers in the world or even see the uniqueness digital photography has to offer.

CHAPTER 1

WHAT IS DIGITAL PHOTOGRAPHY?

Digital photography has more to do with a unique way of taking pictures and not needing a lot of editing features to make it look ideal, as you would want. Some years ago, you would have to take a big camera to a photo shop where the film would need to be taken out and then developed.

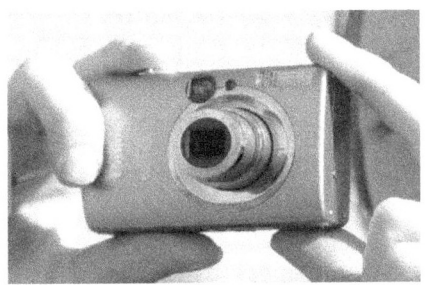

This process mostly took much time and even with that, you didn't have the pictures at your disposal quickly. However, things have changed today with digital photography coming in. When you use a digital camera to take pictures, the elegance and uniqueness is breathtaking and stands out.

Change Your Life With Digital Photography

It wasn't so long ago that people had to take their cameras or the film to a shop to be developed for them. However, all that is needed today is a memory card and pictures on them and everything can be printed out perfectly. Although the very first digital cameras came at a high cost and the quality of pictures weren't so amazing, newer versions are reasonably priced with the best image quality assured. Also, today's digital cameras have many features that make using them simply amazing and so much fun.

Even smart phones are starting to become the best digital cameras for most people. Changing your life with digital photography is now possible. Yes, you can be in style and show your class and style with the different digital photos available in the market today.

If you have not cashed in yet on the exciting offers and features, these digital cameras bring, it is time to start with your smart phones.

Having A Clear Picture Of How Digital Photography Works

If you do not see why there is so much hype about how amazing digital photography is, read on. Digital cameras make it easy for you to share pictures instantly. Also, with these cameras you have the right to keep only the best pictures that you feel look amazing. These images are also very easy to share with all your loved ones, family and the public through Bluetooth, chat messengers, social networks, email, or the internet in general. If you see yourself as a good photographer, try your best to find the best cameras to bring out the uniqueness in the pictures you take.

Renee B. Williams

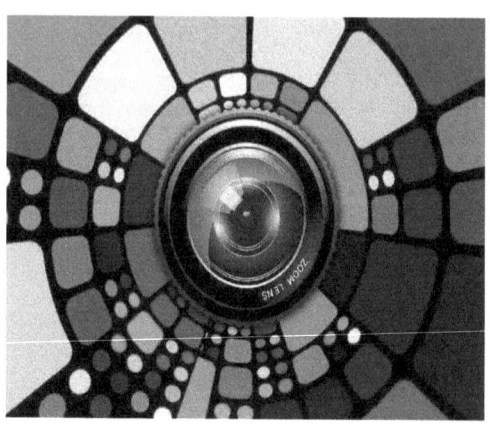

The Uniqueness Of This World Of Photography

The uniqueness of digital photography lies in the quality of pictures that are taken and how flexible taking of pictures has become. Although you might think using them is easy, to take professional pictures you need to be more aware of the different lighting settings and other important factors like the type of camera you are using and the pixels as well. For some years now, there are pictures that have stunned the world with their uniqueness and elegance. The way digital cameras are set to work can be amazing. However, with the features and other settings they are set up with, you can take pictures in black and white, colored, and other exciting color schemes.

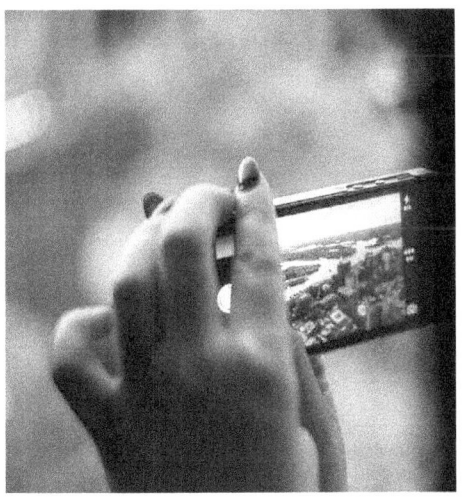

How This World Of Art Helps You Achieve Satisfaction

Pictures have a unique way of telling us about the past. This is why most people love to make good use of digital cameras in taking pictures of important events and memorable times they would want to remember forever. Capturing the ideal moments in our lives some years ago was not as easy as it is today. This is why a lot of people are satisfied today where the world of digital photography is concerned. Today, anyone and everyone can take pictures of their loved ones and of themselves at home and have all the poses they would be shy to take pictures of in public.

CHAPTER 2

SETTING UP A DIGITAL PHOTOGRAPHY BUSINESS

If you have been able to educate yourself in the field of digital art and photography and are planning or ready to set up a business, there will be the need to be strategic about the process. There are so many people who have rushed into the digital photography business only to fail in the end. So, you will need to know exactly what you have that makes you stand out and work that to stay on top. Below are some tips to consider where setting up a digital photography business is concerned;

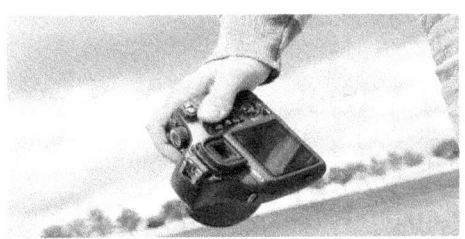

Making The Right Decisions And Choices About Your Field Of Digital Photography

Never rush into making decisions where digital photography is concerned. If you need to learn about the types of digital photography, make sure you get the best teachers to teach you. These days, the world of digital technology has spread its wings. We are all exposed to the very best digital pictures, movies, and songs. No wonder this world of photography is also very popular. The popularity of these digital pictures has risen because it can be sent to loved ones and friends easily. These pictures can also be modified into slide shows, which can be viewed on the monitors of your computer or your TV.

Staying Realistic And Believing In Hard Work

To be an expert, there will be the need to stay realistic and work hard. Working hard is what sums up your credibility as an artiste. The best way to benefit from this field of art is to make use of quality digital cameras. If you are a beginner to the art of digital photography, you can always start by purchasing used digital cameras. They are mostly priced right but you can often find new ones that are affordable as well.

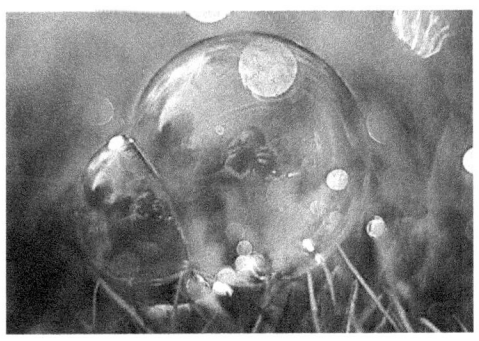

Learning More And On A Daily Basis

Try to learn about anything and everything that relates to what you do. New ideas come from learning more and more. So, the more you learn, the better experience you get to be a better photographer. Being a digital photographer means you need to learn different aspects of photography, such as editing of pictures. Although digital cameras are amazing and provide clear-cut shots, the smoothness of pictures especially those in the pictures you take cannot be assured. This is why you need to learn how to edit pictures in order to clean or erase all unwanted spots from the faces or other parts of the body of the individuals you take pictures of. This will help make the final print out better and more polished.

Some modifications you might need to make include enhancing, cropping, changing shades, getting rid of some imperfections, adjusting picture contrasts, and adding two or more pictures to create new designs. If you are willing to learn, it will be very easy for you to get a grasp on how to use the best photo editing software out there. Although the digital camera is designed with features to make it easier for you to get the best shots, you need to be patient to study how every camera you use works. When you understand a camera, you are able to benefit more from it.

Staying Honest To Your Business And Clients

Be time conscious and never try to treat your clients like they need you more than they do. No matter how big your company gets, it can fall in just a day if your clients stop coming. Know how to relate to and talk to your customers. This will help you a great deal.

Never Make Rush Decisions

In the line of your work, make patience your yardstick. This is the only way you can benefit from your career. Making rush decisions will cause you a lot of pain in the long run. If you want to buy equipment for your office, make sure you search the internet for the best options before any purchase is made. Do not chase cheap brands because you want to save money. Always go for quality no matter what.

Renee B. Williams

Be Ready To Train Others To Work With You

If you are able to reach the top, try your very best to bring others along with you through training. As you train others, you are able to learn more and find out more about other photography. Also, the more you teach, the more you also learn.

CHAPTER 3

HOW DIGITAL PHOTOGRAPHY BENEFITS THE WORLD

Due to digital photography, relationships have blossomed and so many people are able to connect with one another on a more personal level. Just imagine having digital pictures of your childhood printed and designed in an album? How will you feel when you are 20 years old and can still watch those pictures?

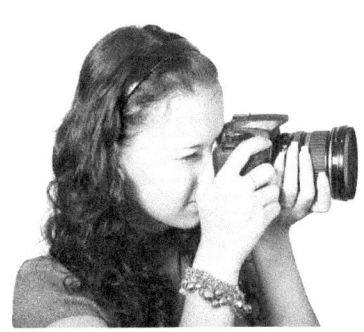

Renee B. Williams

Well, this is one of the unique ways digital photography has affected the world. With this way of photography, you do not need to make any payments to have pictures of your children. Also, you do not need to be worried about the quality of pictures taken if the cameras used are of high quality. Below are some benefits listed that our world today has from the digital world of photography;

- **Living in the moment becomes a possibility**

- **Going back to experience special times in your life becomes easier**

- **You tend to feel safer about tomorrow**

CHAPTER 4

UNDERSTANDING THE 5 W'S OF DIGITAL PHOTOGRAPHY

WHAT

Photography the digital way has been explained in depth in earlier pages. So, read from beginning to know what digital photography is and what is represents in our lives today.

WHO

Who is a digital photographer? A digital photographer is someone who has the training and expertise to take breath-taking pictures with a digital camera. Also, they are able to take the best shots by combining various elements to make sure the pictures they take come out perfectly.

WHEN

Digital photography makes it easy for the best moments of life to be captured every single second of the day. Where a digital camera is concerned, all you need is the right shot and you will have a perfect picture in no time.

WHERE

Digital pictures can be taken everywhere you go. All you need is your digital camera and the right motivation to take memorable pictures. There are however times when the place you take pictures affects the quality of the picture you are taking even with the best digital cameras. This is why you need to be very careful. If the pictures you are taken are professional or are for a professional purpose, you will be better off taking them with the right lighting, backgrounds and also to suit the preference of what it will be used for.

WHOM

Digital Photography

Anyone can take digital pictures even with their smart phones. However, if you are not able to do so with your smart phone and you have a digital camera, it will be perfect. With the best digital camera brands, you do not need any special techniques to shoot normal pictures in the right settings. This means, you just need the motivation and you will be taking beautiful pictures of your family and friends in no time.

CHAPTER 5

DIGITAL PHOTOGRAPHY FOR FUN

Taking digital pictures for fun can be so exciting. However, you need to take quality pictures even if you are taking them for fun. This helps to make you feel better about yourself and makes it very easy for you to consider taking it as a career if you realize you are exceptionally good in this artistic field.

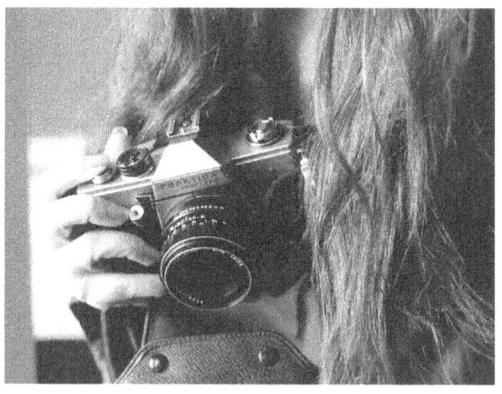

Most professional photographers today started photography for fun. Below

Digital Photography

are some tips to take into consideration where fun digital photography is concerned;

- **Make sure you own a good digital camera**

- **Try to read a little about taking good pictures**

- **Make sure you have a hard disk drive where all pictures are kept**

- **Never cease a moment to take a life-transforming photograph**

CHAPTER 6

DIGITAL PHOTOGRAPHY FOR EVENTS

Events are the basis upon which our world is built. Every single day there are different events that happen in the lives of many people. Although the previous way of taking pictures made it difficult for many photographs to be taken, the digital age of photography has changed so many things.

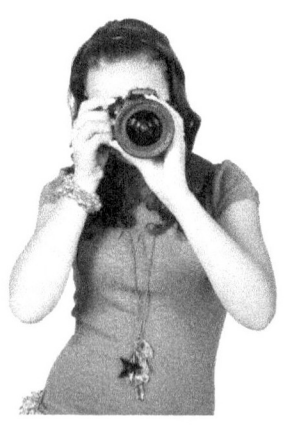

Digital Photography

Today, there are so many people who take their digital cameras along with them to all events they attend to get shots of the best moments. This has helped to make it very easy for people to build and keep memories. Below are some of the events that are commonly held in our world today.

Weddings

There is no way any wedding ceremony will be complete without the right photographs. Due to digital cameras, it is very easy to have all pictures of your wedding taken easily and even printed on the spot for you if you want to have them. There are specific moments during the wedding ceremony like when the couple is saying their vows, wearing their rings, kissing, dancing, etc. that you might want to have exclusives of. With your digital camera, you can take these pictures for free at your own will. Couples hire expert digital photographers to cover the whole event on their behalf as they take pictures of the event from start to finish. This shows how valuable digital photographers have become over the years.

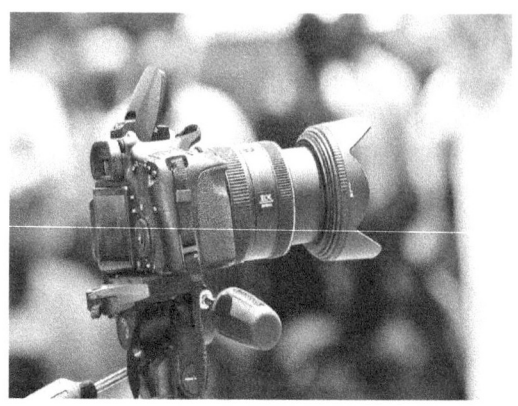

Corporate Parties

Corporate parties take place all year round all over the world. This is why having a digital camera you can use to take pictures of these events when you attend helps. You can use these pictures to count down the line how far you have come in a company and also check to find out if there are any changes that you see from the past and now where your looks are concerned. Companies also hire the services of photographers to take pictures of such events to add to their company album to know how far they have come as a company.

Birthday Parties

Birthday parties are celebrated every single day of every year all around the world. So digital cameras all over the world are always busy taking pictures of the celebrant and also the cake, pictures of friends, families, etc.

Having a birthday party, without pictures after the party is like never having one at all. This is why all types of digital cameras are made present by the friends and family of the celebrant as well as expert photographers hired for the day. Just imagine, adding one more year to your life without any health problems, this is indeed the day to make merry and be grateful.

Concerts

Digital cameras are perfect for taking pictures of your favorite artists and other stars at concerts you attend.

Graduations

Graduations are memorable and the best pictures need to be kept to tell your story one day. This is why digital photographers are hired for such occasions every single day of the week in all parts of the world.

Funerals

Naming Ceremonies

CHAPTER 7

BUILDING YOUR CONFIDENCE AS A DIGITAL PHOTOGRAPHER

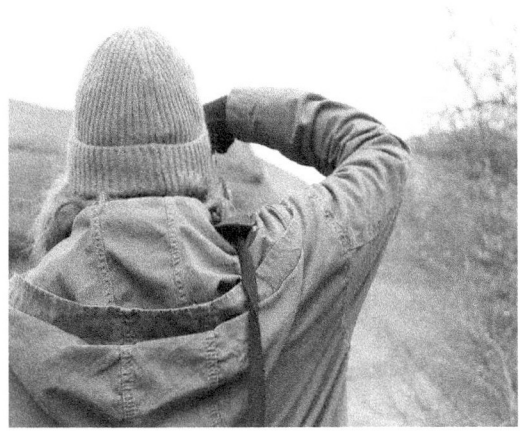

- Learn more to acquire more knowledge

- Believe you are the best and have the best to offer

- **Try to have something unique about the pictures you take**

- **Make sure you know how to edit pictures very well too**

- **Treat others with respect no matter what**

CHAPTER 8

DIGITAL PHOTOGRAPHY CAMERAS

If you view yourself as a professional photographer, you should know exactly the type of camera you will need to take breathtaking shots? Do you need to invest in DSLR? An easy to use digital camera is perfect for the amateur photographers.

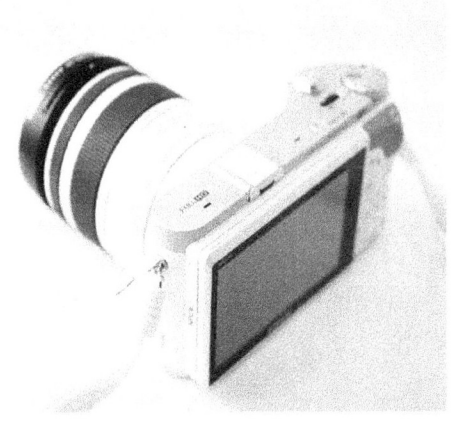

Knowing about all these different cameras will help you in making the right decision. Before anything though, it will be best to know that for professional digital photography, DSLRs are the best option. Always check mount compatibility before you buy any digital camera.

Benefits Of Using High Quality Cameras

There is the SLR camera to begin with. If you do not know what these cameras are but have seen professional and difficult to use cameras mostly used by expert photographers these are called SLR and DSLR cameras. SLR is an abbreviation for Single Lens Reflex. These cameras make it easy for photographers to witness just what their cameras are seeing when they look through the viewfinder. Cheaper cameras use two different lenses. One lens is for the real camera and the other is used for the viewfinder. This impacts the way pictures come out altogether, especially where close-up shots are concerned.

Then, there is also the DSLR camera. Digital Single-Lens Reflex cameras are slightly different than SLR cameras. A DSLR camera helps the photographers see exactly what the complete or final picture will look like. Image preview on screen including viewfinder lenses is a helpful feature for DSLR camera users.

The benefits of using DSLR cameras are countless. Due to the improvement in technology and fall in prices, a high quality DSLR is within reach for enthusiastic amateurs. They produce exceptional picture quality and more creative pictures compared to compact cameras.

One main advantage of DSLR is that you are able to use transposable lenses to create diverse effects like a wide-angle lens for striking panoramic shots, telephoto lens for zooming-in from long angles, or macro lenses for capturing small objects. You can as well make use of different accessories like different flashes and tripods to improve your picture taking experience.

Where To Find Information About Different Digital Cameras

The internet is one of the best places where you can find detailed information on digital cameras. All you need is to find the right websites and also find out the detailed information they have to offer you. Make sure you use more than one website. This way, you will be able to get results from all sides, which help a lot.

Cameras For Professional And Hobby Pictures

Using high quality digital cameras can be the best alternative for you no matter what. This is because you can count on having exceptional shots when you use high quality cameras. Learning more about the different cameras available for professional and hobby use will make it easier for you to understand what to look out for when you need to buy high quality cameras and also the benefits they offer. Whether you want to take professional or hobby pictures, you need to make sure the camera you use is of high quality. This helps to turn even your hobby pictures into stunners.

DSLR cameras are good for enthusiasts who love to delve into all the technical details of photography. Compact cameras are good for those who want to take better pictures, but do not have the money to buy the expensive detailed cameras.

Smartphone Cameras

Smartphone cameras are considered the best cameras for capturing quick pictures that can be edited quickly and also shared online. Some years ago, mobile phones that could take pictures provided users with small, grainy pictures, which allowed users to see almost nothing of what they wanted. Although they were handy where taking and sharing photos quickly was concerned, they were not perfect for taking the right pictures that you could print with large outcomes or at large sizes.

This has however changed today. Today, manufacturers of Smartphone have found out ways to squeeze lots of technology into a small phone. Some phones for instant have to up to 41 megapixels. This is better than most of the cheap digital cameras available in the market. One other major issue with camera phones in the past was that, they were simply used as fixed focus and digital zooming cameras, which made it difficult to take close up shots and long-range pictures. However, digital cameras for instance come with full optical zoom lenses that make zooming in and out so much fun.

Compact Digital Cameras

With compact digital cameras you just point and then shoot. Even if you feel DSLR cameras are too complex, then a compact digital camera might be the best for you. These types of cameras are easier to use. Most of the camera types let you play with settings and other features like exposure or shutter speed, and other pre-set shooting modes like portrait mode, action, nighttime, etc.

If you want you can decide to leave everything on auto setting and allow the camera do its own magic. These cameras fit perfectly well into pockets or bags. Also, they are easy to use and give you the required outcomes. Below are some unique features of compact digital cameras;

RESOLUTION

The quality of pictures that are taken with digital camera is based on the resolution of the camera, which is measured is MP or megapixels. Digital images are made up of millions of colored, minute squares known as pixels. The more pixels the digital camera has, the sharper the pictures taken. A high-resolution camera will be able to give you the ability to crop all pictures without losing much detail.

DIGITAL OR OPTICAL ZOOM

Compact cameras generally come with two unique ways of zooming-in pictures for close up shots, which are the optical and digital zoom. Optical zoom mostly makes use of lenses to expand the photos, and therefore pictures do not lose their quality. Digital zoom also cuts out and expands the center of pictures, which leads to reduction of its quality. Try your best to buy digital cameras with optimal zoom.

STORAGE

Your pictures will be saved on memory cards. The capacity of the cards is mostly measured in gigabytes and megabytes. The higher the memory card capacity level, the more pictures you can save on them.

CHAPTER 9

DIGITAL PHOTOGRAPHY IN ALL INDUSTRIES

Today, digital photography has entered all industries all over the world. This is not because it is a new way of photography that needs to be accepted, it is because digital photography is unique. Understanding the uniqueness of this world of photography however can be seen when you scroll through an album of beautiful pictures taken in today's digital age and those that were taken some 25 or even 40 years ago.

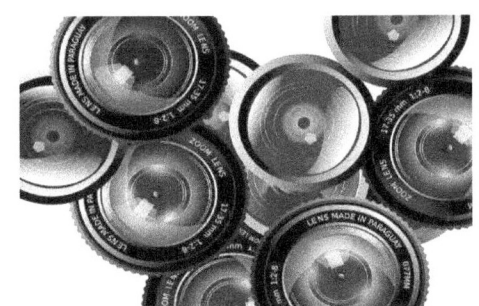

News And Reporting Media

Renee B. Williams

Some years ago, photographers assigned to newspapers had to wait for their film rolls to be sent for processing before their pictures could be printed in their newspapers. Because all photographs were captured with cameras that used 35mm films, photographers would need to create their very own pictures for inclusion, or make sure they were sent for development quickly. At this time, photographers had to pray for their pictures to come back on time so that they would be able to submit before deadline.

However, the world of technology as always has made things better today in the news and reporting media with digital photography. Today, digital photographers can take pictures, edit them and send them through their emails in matter of seconds. This is especially important to sports news reporters who love to have up-to-date action pictures on hand to link them with their match articles and reports.

Health

One other aspect of our lives that has greatly benefited from digital photography's introduction to the world is the health and medical industry. Thanks to the introduction of digital images, taking scans and x-rays are easily done today and can be shared with surgeons, specialists and other local health practitioners, across a country and even all over the world. Also, these images can be saved or stored electronically on hard drives. This means, they are safely kept and will not take up needed storage space in some dusty and dirty basement.

Social Media

Through the uniqueness of digital photography, taking and sharing pictures with friends and family all over the world has become possible. Some years ago, you would have to wait for your film to be developed and printed out before you could post them off to your loved ones. However, digital pictures can be sent easily today through social media. Today, you do not need to waste money on having films developed and pictures printed before enlarging them again, and then sending to distant relatives, etc. All you need is the internet and you can connect your digital camera cable to your computer and send as many pictures as possible.

Entertainment

After major concerts and events are over, having the pictures of the event instantly has become possible today. Some years ago, the same film developing process was needed to make things a reality. However, it is not the same today due to digital cameras.

CHAPTER 10

SOME DIGITAL PHOTOGRAPHY TYPES

If you have been thinking of pursuing a career in digital photography, then there are so many opportunities for you to tap into. All over the world, digital photography is fast becoming very popular, with different paths to make your choice from. If you have an interest in taking on the world of digital photography, and would love to learn more about the alternatives you have, then reading this Book is the best decision you ever made.

Knowing the different types of digital photography is the first step to starting your journey into this whole new, but exciting world of digital photography. A lot of people fail to understand these types of photography and it goes a long way to derail them.

All of these digital photography types however can be linked or combined together by one person. Yes, it is very possible and many photographers are making that happen. The world of photography provides you with a wide variety of alternatives where career path is concerned. So, it is up to you to decide which ones when combined will be best for you and also how you can make the most out of your career. Try to get basic training first in all types and then you can choose which one will be better for you.

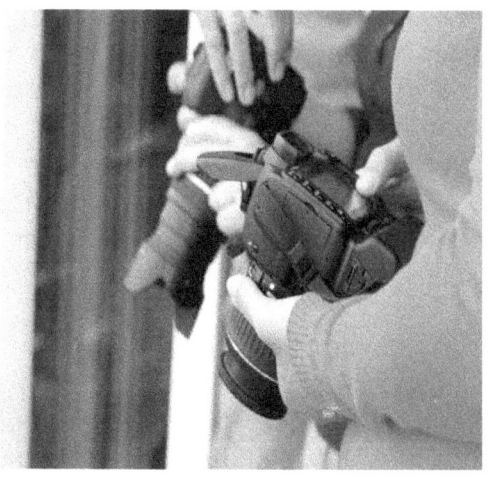

Portrait Photography

Digital Photography

Portrait photography is the very first type of digital photography you will need to know about in your journey to discover the different types of photography in the digital world. This type of photography is one of the most popular types that attract many people. Mostly, you will see portrait photographers in photography sections of big and small photography shops taking passport pictures, graduation pictures, individual pictures and also family pictures. This type of photography can be so much fun and profitable if you tackle it very well.

Landscape And Travel Photography

For those who love to travel or love to work outside, landscape of travel photography is another type of digital photography you can definitely try. Unlike the portrait type that is kind of stagnant to a location, the landscape and travel photography type takes you around and you get to take pictures from different travel locations, etc. Landscape photographers create memorable scenes. They use colors, angles, and lights to create these memorable scenes. Landscape photographers are able to easily draw their audience into their world of art and this is what makes them stand out.

Travel photography however has to do more with bringing people into your world of art by taking pictures of breathtaking moments that express the people, and culture of specific countries and places. Travel photography can be taken or seen as a full time or part time job or even as a hobby. So, if you love travelling and take great digital pictures, then you should make it a must to take pictures of the places you visit and all the beautiful cultural scenes you want to share with the world. You can definitely sell these pictures for more money.

Wildlife Photography

If you love animals and love to know more about their way of life or have beautiful pictures of them, you may want to consider taking a shot at wildlife photography. Wildlife photography is another world or type of digital photography. Being a wildlife photographer can be very exciting and rewarding as well. However, based on the wildlife type you decide to capture, the level of risk can be minimum or very high.

Wildlife photographers have been known over the years to put themselves in very risky situations just to bring the world the unique pictures they are able to take. This happens because to get the best shots, getting closer to most of the animals are paramount and this is mostly a very dangerous thing.

If you have an interest in the world of wildlife photography, make sure you enroll in a training course to make sure you are 100% sure of all the risks involves as well as how you can protect yourself in the process. Above all that, this type of photography is simply amazing.

Fashion Photography

If you love fashion, style and all the glamour it comes with, then you will definitely love the world of fashion photography. Today, there are so many fashion photographers in the world and this is not because it is an easy field to choose, it is because fashion simply attracts more and more people.

Breaking into the fashion industry as a photographer however can be very difficult unless you have some unique style with the photographs you take. As soon as you settle, you get to benefit from the attractive monetary compensations it comes with which is real. A fashion photographer needs to have many traits like passion for fashion, ability to take breathtaking portrait pictures, and also the ability to sell or market brands or products through the pictures he or she takes.

CHAPTER 11

UNDERSTANDING WHAT PIXELS ARE IN THE WORLD OF DIGITAL PHOTOGRAPHY

Some years ago, artwork was made and created with paints, dyes, pigments and inks. However, as we have gradually moved and landed into the digital world, artworks we knew in the past are being shifted into the digital way especially where photography is concerned – the pixel. Today, every digital creation no matter what form they come in is composed of pixels. However, what are these pixels?

Pixel is the short word for 'picture element'. So, to be clear, pixels are one of the many little details or even elements that create the complete image. Every picture or digital piece of art is made up of pixels. This means, the more pixels a picture has, the bigger and more unique the artwork involved will likely be.

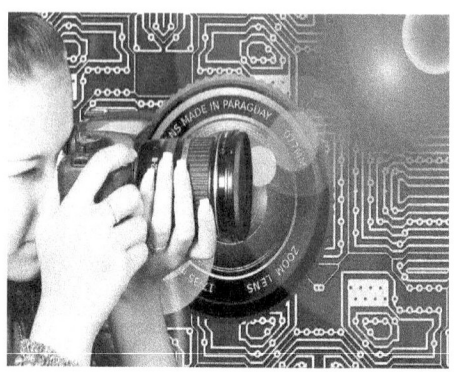

The Internet Can Be The Best Resource Tool For You

When you read the internet, it becomes very easy to find out more about pixels and digital photography in totality. For instance, you will be able to learn that 'resolution' is the number of pixels that are used to create images. The best digital cameras in the market can mostly be determined by pixel counts. This is because the larger the pixel count, the better quality of pictures they take.

In colored pictures or images, pixels mostly comprise of three main colors called RGB (red, green and blue) or even four-color dots called CMYK (cyan, magenta, yellow and black). Most of the digital images available today are saved as RGB due to the way their screens are programmed to read colors and bring out the light.

Read More Books On Digital Photography

Reading more books on digital photography makes it very easy for you to understand this world of art better. Apart from pixels, there are megapixels as well. Reading more will make it easier for you to have a clear idea what they all stand for and represent. This will help to improve your photography experience and make you a happier person.

What Are Megapixels?

These days, most of the focus is on megapixels far more than it is on individual pixels. When you see 1,000,000 pixels you should know it is a megapixel. Additionally, it also portrays the number of image sensor elements in the digital camera. In most of the digital cameras on the market today, sensor arrays are covered with patterned color filter mosaics that contain RGB.

Although megapixels are big and offer more, there is no way pictures will have the classy look they do when taken with digital cameras if pixels are not involved working their magic. So, make sure the digital cameras you buy have the highest pixels ever.

CHAPTER 12

BE OPEN MINDED TO NEW IDEAS

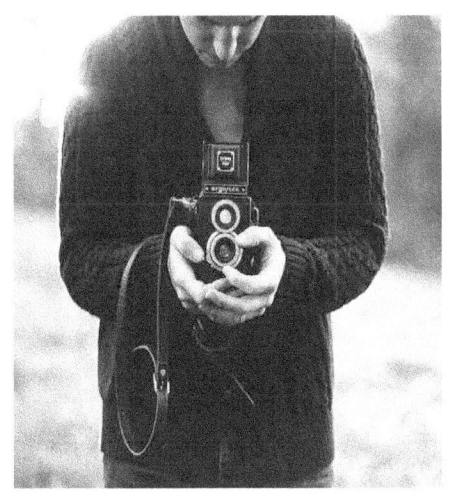

- **Try new stuff to expand your creativity**

- **Try to work with others**

- **Try to see a unique opportunity in all pictures you take**

- **Understand lighting where digital photos are concerned**

CHAPTER 13

LEARNING DIGITAL PHOTOGRAPHY

So, is it important to learn the art of digital photography if you want to be an expert in the field? Well, the answer to this question is yes. It is true that you might have heard many stories of people who just chanced into the career without receiving training from any school.

The truth about these professionals is that, although they started with their own ideas and thoughts, they have gradually grown into it. Yes, they take classes along the line to become perfect and also to know more about the new technologies in the industry.

Even these experts believe in the power learning more brings or has to offer. So, you should also be psyched to learn. Today, you can decide to learn digital photography online or in your area. Everything depends on you so, make the right decision.

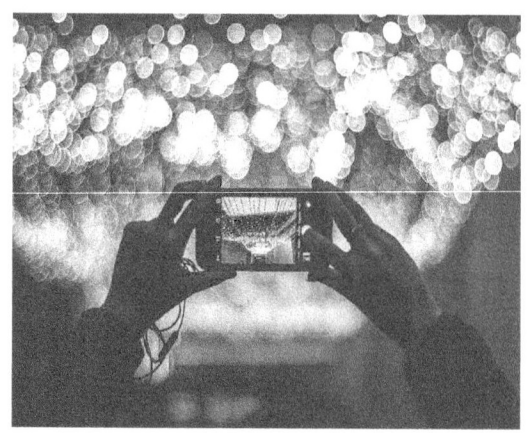

Online Digital Photography Classes

What are online digital photography classes? Well, knowing more about online digital photography classes is as easy as ABCD. With more and more people taking digital photography as a hobby on a daily basis, the need to separate the men from the boys come in where professionalism is shown. What makes the digital photography art beautiful is that all you need to start is a digital camera.

With digital cameras being very affordable today, you can relax and count on buying one from an online store or an area in your shop or store. Apart from having your digital camera, you will need some added skills and training for you to take the best pictures. This is why aspiring photographers always look for a way to improve their skills in picture taking.

Although taking an offline course in your local university is the best way out, it will be better if you take an online course first. This is because online classes tend to be cheaper and very opportune. You will have the opportunity to learn on your very own time.

Choosing The Right Courses

Before you even choose the right digital photography courses for you, there will be the need to look for the courses online. Searching for 'online digital photography courses' in a popular search engine is the best way to begin your search. With this search, you get a long list of results, which you can make your selections from.

Nevertheless, before you make a decision with regards to your course, make sure you research about the courses and also the institutions you want to learn with. This will help you make the right decision as to which course is the best for you and also the right learning center online as well.

Paying The Right Amount For The Education You Get

When you search for the right digital photography online courses for you, there will be the need for you to be certain you are choosing the right online institution and that you are paying the right amount. This can be done by comparing the different websites and finding out their cost structure as well as the facilities they offer to students. This helps to give you the very best value for money even with the best courses and tutoring benefits.

Digital Photography

Most online classes for the different digital courses will begin by teaching you the foundation of digital photography. As soon as you have the foundations down, you are moved to learn more advanced methods in the digital lighting world like image editing, lighting, and adjusting tone.

No matter your current level of experience, online courses help to add up and perfect your skills. Also, you get to meet other photographers from all parts of the world and have the best communication to share ideas as well as build new relationships.

Read Online Reviews To Help You Decide

In deciding which online digital photography schools will be the best for you, you can begin your search by looking for private websites, which review online digital photography schools and courses. With these sites, you will be able to see how their ratings go and also if a particular course or school will be best for you or not.

Online reviews have a unique way of helping you make the right decisions. However, you still need to follow them with much care. Try your best to read more than 3 review sites before you draw a conclusion. Concluding your search with just one review site is a mistake you will live to regret. If reviews of a specific school or course have favorable reviews on more than 3 websites, then you can decide to settle with them. You can shortlist up to five courses and schools for appraisal.

Always Compare Different Online Teaching Sites

When you make your shortlist of schools and courses try to compare the different facilities all these schools have and also how their teaching methods are like. Compare everything you can from course length, time for lectures, books and resources made available, etc. All of these add up to determining the credibility of the online school and also the courses you will be learning.

Free Online Digital Photography Courses

Although most online digital photography courses will require you to make some payments, there are some that are for free. However, with most of the free courses you get to benefit only from basic information and will not get detailed information and techniques. However, if you do not have money, but still want to learn you can always try the free digital photography online courses first.

At least, you will still be learning some things that you need to spearhead your digital photography career that you were never aware of in the past. As you benefit from these free courses, you can save money to further with the advanced courses to take your skills to a better level.

FAQ

Should I take my love for digital photography seriously?

Yes. You should take it seriously and try to obtain training in becoming a professional. No one knows where you might end up in few years from now.

How do I know I am meant to work in this industry?

There is no special sign that tells you if you are meant to be in the industry or not. All you should have is your love for photography, your confidence and preparedness to make the most out of this artistic world. When you take pictures and receive the best recommendations and realize your love for this art is growing by the day, you should consider taking it more seriously.

Why should I charge reasonably when my competition is charging high prices?

Digital Photography

You are not your competition. Maybe you get the clients you do because you charge reasonably. So, why will you want to go high because someone else is doing the same? If you need to increase the cost of your services for another reason which is linked to making your business bigger and making it work, then that is fine. However, never try to run your photography center on what your competitors do.

I have clients who always want something different. What do I do?

These clients will always walk into your offices or call you. However, do not be bothered. All you need to do is to work very hard to please them and if it will take you to research and find out more about what they want online, just do it to please them. This is what it takes to be the best.

A client got angry with my final work on her pictures, what do I do?

Discuss with her and even if she is wrong, agree she is right. Try to calm her down. After you are able to do that, tell her you are sorry and give her a new offer to take new pictures all over again at no cost. This will definitely make any client happy. Be patient with clients because they sell your company to the world through their reviews.

Should I ask for help from fellow photographers when I find things difficult?

There are times when your competition is your enemy. However, if you have friends in the photography world that you know will be more than happy to share their experiences and advice sometimes there will be the need to contact them. There is nothing wrong in asking people what you have no idea about. This helps to build your mind and also makes you gain respect in the eyes of those you go to.

Are highly priced digital cameras better than cheap ones?

Digital Photography

The answer to this question cannot be a complete yes or no. This is because a lot of expensive digital cameras are expensive for nothing. You will need to find the right camera with the right pixels and other features before you can get the best shots you need. The prices however will depend on your budget and how much you are willing and ready to spend.

My daughter loves to take and edit pictures during family events, should I encourage her?

Definitely, encouraging her is the best gift you can ever give her.

Where can I buy the best digital camera from?

The internet has so many stores you can buy the best digital cameras from. However, make sure you buy from the best online store and also make sure you do not take online review sites for granted in any purchase you make.

How do I know the best digital camera when I see one?

The best digital camera will have the specific features you need to have the high-resolution pictures you need. Here, brand names do not really matter.

Digital Photography

DISCLAIMER

This Book offers the readers an insight into the world of digital photography, added details about this artistic industry. It does not contain or has duplicated contents copied from any other source, book or site. The owner of the book should be contacted if anyone, site or writer wants to use partial/all content present in this Book for personal or commercial purposes.

All content provided in this Book are unique to this website alone. The website does not make any warranties, uttered, and therefore disowns and cancels all other warranties, in addition to without restraint, warranties that are indirect or merchantability conditions, or added intrusion of rights.

Moreover, the website doesn't call for or makes any illustrations concerning the accuracy, reliability of the use of all content on the site, likely results, if not linking to any such materials or on any other website/s the site is linked to.

Renee B. Williams

ABOUT AUTHOR

Hi, I am Renee B. Williams. I'm a writer and I love to read and write about networking and security systems. I read so many books on networking and technologies. I'm a fast learner and I have knowledge of different networking programs and security systems and hacking as well. I am so much passionate about learning new things. The main reason why I am writing books is I want to let others know about hacking and security systems in a simple and easy way to understand. I have vast knowledge on the best and fastest ways to learning. So, I decided to write my own courses in the form of kindle books, where you can learn quickly and easily how to use security systems.